Arts and Crafts
of
ANCIENT CHINA

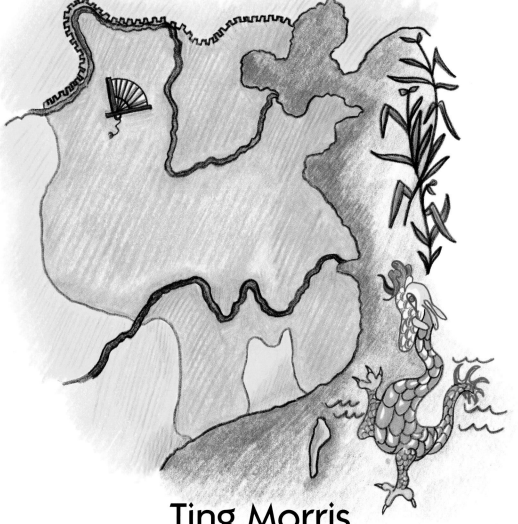

Ting Morris

Illustrated by Emma Young

A+

Smart Apple Media

Published by Smart Apple Media
2140 Howard Drive West, North Mankato, MN 56003

Artwork by Emma Young
Designed by Helen James
Edited by Mary-Jane Wilkins
Picture research by Su Alexander

Photograph acknowledgements
Front cover Asian Art & Archaeology, Inc./Corbis; 5t Lowell Georgia/Corbis,
b Werner Forman/Corbis; 6 & 7 Asian Art & Archaeology, Inc./Corbis; 8
Royal Ontario Museum/Corbis; 9t Christie's Images/Corbis, b Asian Art &
Archaeology, Inc./Corbis; 10 Copyright the Trustees of The British Museum;
12 Bettmann/Corbis; 13t Archivo Iconografico, S.A./Corbis, b Werner
Forman/Corbis; 14 Wolfgang Kaehler/Corbis; 15 Royal Ontario Museum/
Corbis; 16 Liu Liqun/Corbis; 18 Tibor Bognar/Corbis; 19 Werner Forman/
Corbis; 20t Robert Pickett/Corbis, b Burstein Collection/Corbis; 21 Christie's
Images/Corbis; 22 Blue Lantern Studio/Corbis; 24 Kimbell Art Museum/
Corbis; 25 & 26 Copyright the Trustees of The British Museum; 27 Macduff
Everton/Corbis; 28 Asian Art & Archaeology, Inc./Corbis

Printed in Singapore

Library of Congress Cataloging-in-Publication Data

Morris, Ting.
Ancient China / by Ting Morris.
p. cm. — (Arts and crafts of the ancient world)
Includes index.
ISBN-13: 978-1-58340-914-5
1. Handicraft—China—History—Juvenile literature. 2. China—Social life
and customs—History—Juvenile literature. I. Title. II. Series

TT101.M67 2006
680.931—dc22 2005037714

First Edition

9 8 7 6 5 4 3 2 1

Contents

The world of the ancient Chinese

Ancient Chinese civilization grew near two great rivers. Around 9,000 years ago, people started growing cereals such as millet near the banks of the Huang He (Yellow River). The river's name came from the color of its mud, which spread across the land when the river flooded. This made fertile fields for growing crops.

Further south there was more rainfall. Here an even bigger river called Chang Jiang (Long River) flowed through the landscape. This area was ideal for growing rice. Over thousands of years, small farming villages near both rivers grew into towns and cities.

Around 2000 B.C., powerful rulers had taken control of the land we now call China. According to Chinese legend, the first rulers belonged to a dynasty called Xia. By the time they came to power, Chinese artists and craftworkers were making attractive clay pots and casting useful bronze tools.

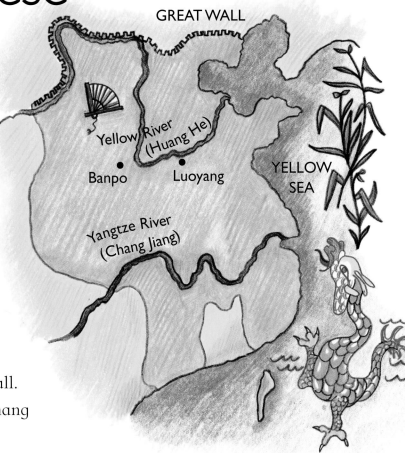

The first ruler of a united Chinese empire came to power in 221 B.C. This map shows the size of the empire (in green).

Village of early potters

Historians call the first ancient Chinese civilization the Yangshao culture. People lived in farming villages beside the Yellow River, where they grew millet and kept pigs. Archaeologists uncovered the remains of a village called Banpo, and to their surprise, they found a pottery-making area outside of the village.

The first Banpo pots were made at least 6,000 years ago. These are from the excavated village. Archaeologists have glued the broken pots together.

Here craftsmen had shaped their clay pots by hand. The potters' area included six kilns in which the pots were baked until they were hard. After firing the pots, artists added black designs to the red clay surface.

Cave temples

Buddhist missionaries from India first brought their religion to China around A.D. 150. Merchants followed and brought their own ideas about sculpture and painting, which influenced Chinese artists. By the fourth century, Buddhism was the main religion, and Chinese sculptors began carving cave temples. In the cliffs beside a river near the city of Luoyang, they carved 100,000 Buddhist images onto 2,000 caves. The sculptures were carved straight from the caves' gray limestone rock. The art of cave sculpture lasted until the ninth century.

These carved statues of disciples and divine beings stand in one of the "Longmen" (or "Dragon Gate") caves near Luoyang.

Bronze casting

Bronze is a mixture of copper and tin. It was a very important metal to the ancient Chinese, who started using it more than 4,000 years ago for tools, ceremonial pots, and ornaments.

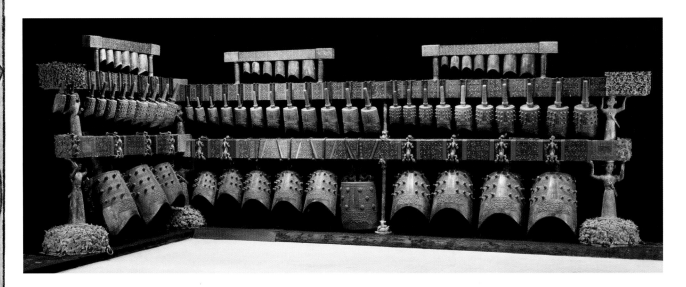

Before Buddhism arrived from India, the Chinese used bronze items as offerings to their ancestors. At first, they hammered the bronze into shape. Later, they cast the metal in clay molds. First, they made a clay model of the object. When this had hardened, they packed more clay around it to make the mold.

This musical instrument has 64 bronze bells. Each one played a different note when it was struck with a wooden stick.

They baked the mold in a kiln and then heated bronze until it was melted and runny. They poured the bronze into the mold and left it to harden. Many different craftsmen worked on each stage of this process. Archaeologists have found fine examples of their skillful work. The tomb of a nobleman, who died around 433 B.C., contained eight tons (10 t) of bronze, including a complete set of musical bells (shown above).

Ding, gong and pan

Metalworkers would cast large containers in sections, then put them together. These bronze containers had names. A "ding" was a big round pot, with two handles and three legs, used for serving cooked food. A "gong" was a wine jug with a decorated lid. A "pan" was a shallow basin for water. Sets of pots were buried with their owners so they could offer food and drink to their ancestors.

Heavenly horses

In 139 B.C., the emperor of the Western Han dynasty sent an envoy to central Asia. The envoy was to find people to help the Chinese fight the nomads threatening their northern borders. When he reached the region of Ferghana (modern Uzbekistan), the envoy saw sleek, fast horses that he described as heavenly. Soon the Chinese were sending large amounts of silk to Ferghana in exchange for horses. Metalworkers cast models of these prized animals.

This bronze model of a horse was made during the Western Han period (206 B.C.–A.D. 9).

Stone of the heavens

The ancient Chinese treasured jade and called it "the stone of the heavens." It consists of a mineral called nephrite, which is found in a wide range of colors, from green and gray to red and black. Their favorite color was emerald green, which became known as "imperial jade."

At first, craftsmen used jade to make tools and weapons. Many of these were probably designed to be used in ceremonies, rather than for practical purposes. Later, they carved delicate jade figurines, ornaments, and jewelry. Nephrite is sometimes called soft jade (there is also a harder variety called jadeite) and it is difficult to work. Ancient Chinese craft workers were very skillful, and made small, finely carved objects.

Mysterious disks

Beginning in 3800 B.C., the ancient Chinese put disks of jade into graves and tombs. Many of the disks, which are known as *bi*, were more than eight inches (20 cm) wide, and had a circular hole in the middle. The craftsmen who made the *bi* usually polished them and sometimes carved designs on both sides.

This is a group of jade pendants, with the oldest at the top. The mask and rooster were made around 1200 B.C. The three pendants in the middle are in the shape of dragons, which were famous mythological beasts in China. The cats at the bottom were made around 400 B.C.

In some tombs, many jade disks were placed around the bodies of the dead. We do not know why they were put there. Perhaps they were part of the burial ceremony, or were used to guard against demon spirits and helped a person's soul live forever.

This smooth, polished *bi* may be 3,000 years old.

Burial suits

In 1968, archaeologists opened a pair of ancient tombs about 93 miles (150 km) southwest of Beijing, the capital of China. The tombs were cut into the rock of a hillside and inside were treasures made of bronze and gold. The tombs were made around 113 B.C. for the Chinese emperor's son Liu Sheng and his wife, Princess Tou Wan. The royal couple were buried in suits made of thousands of small pieces of jade, which were sewn together with gold wire. They probably thought that the jade would preserve their bodies after death and protect their souls on the journey to the afterlife.

The burial suit of Princess Tou Wan contains 2,150 small plates of jade.

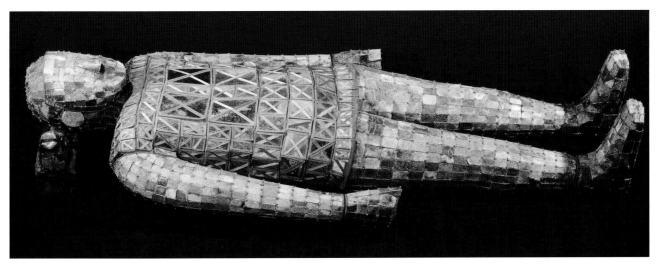

Make a monster face

Chinese artists carved small jade faces and masks that were half-human, half-animal. We do not know what these were for, but they were very popular and have become collectors' items.

You can make look-alike jade carvings using transparent modeling clay, which you can buy in toy or craft stores. Or, you can make them from homemade salt dough.

A Chinese craftsman carved this monster face from jade about 4,000 years ago.

Make a jade face

You will need: 1 cup flour • 1 cup salt • 6–8 tablespoons water • 1 teaspoon cooking oil • green food coloring or paint • thin cardboard • a rolling pin • a modeling tool • a toothpick • a non-stick baking tray • varnish.

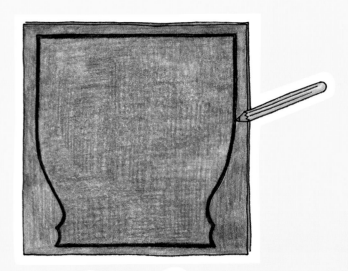

1 Copy the monster's head and neck outline onto the cardboard and cut it out.

2 Put the flour in a mixing bowl and stir in the salt. Color the water with a tiny drop of green food coloring and add the oil. Slowly stir the liquid into the dry ingredients. Knead for 5 to 10 minutes, until the dough is smooth. If it's dry, add water. If it's sticky, add flour.

3 Roll out about half the dough to about one-half inch (1 cm) thick. Lay the cardboard template on it and cut around it. This is the base for your face.

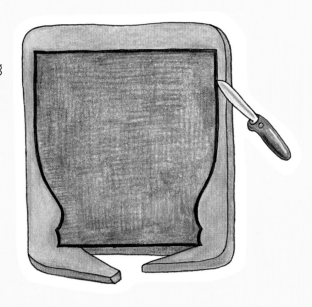

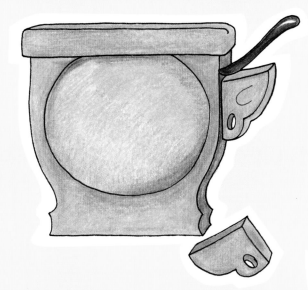

4 Pat a ball of dough into a face shape. Roll out more dough and cut a long strip about one-half inch (1 cm) wide for the hair. Cut several smaller strips to shape into ears. Moisten the base with a little water and press on the face and hair. Stick on the ears, smoothing the joints with your finger. Shape the chin and hairline with a modeling tool.

5 Use a toothpick to mark the hair. Model eyes, eyebrows, nose, and mouth from balls and strips of dough. Don't forget the monster's sharp teeth!

6 Put the face on a baking tray and place on the bottom rack of an oven at 275 °F (140 °C) for 30 minutes. Turn the oven down to 200 °F (110 °C) and leave for 30 minutes more, or until dry. When the model has cooled, varnish it to look like glossy jade. Take care of your face—jade gives courage and drives away evil.

11

Painting styles

The earliest Chinese paintings found were made on silk during the early part of the Western Han dynasty (206 B.C.–A.D. 9). They were banners used in burials to cover and line wooden coffins.

Painters wanted a very smooth surface. They used the finest silk, but their inks dripped and blurred the picture, so they coated the silk with a thin layer of a gluey substance. Early artists preferred to paint on silk rather than paper, which may have been invented around the same time and may have been very rough. Many artists painted mountains because they were thought to be sacred places. The natural landscape was the subject of many paintings, not just a background for other subjects.

Rules of behavior

Some paintings were done to show people how to behave, rather than to be beautiful to look at. Words of praise were written on paintings of great heroes, and young people were shown respecting their parents. At court and elsewhere, young women were expected to behave correctly and gracefully.

This painted silk banner is more than 6 feet (2 m) long. It lined a coffin in a tomb built around 180 B.C. The painter shows three worlds: the underworld (at the bottom), the everyday world, and the heavenly world of the gods and spirits (at the top).

This is a seventh-century copy of one of Gu Khaizi's instructive paintings. It shows a teacher writing down rules of behavior for two young women at the imperial court.

One of the great painters of this style was Gu Khaizi, who lived in the fourth century A.D. He painted a long silk scroll with pictures showing correct behavior at the imperial court. Other artists copied this style in later times.

Ink shading

Another Chinese style was *baihua*, meaning, "white painting." In this style, the artist used shades of one ink color instead of many different colors.

One of the famous painters of this style was Han Gan, who lived in the eighth century A.D. His favorite subject was horses. He was such a good painter that the emperor asked him to paint the horses in the imperial stables. Animals were popular subjects for paintings, especially horses with fiery tempers. Some people believed they were dragons in disguise.

This painting on silk by Han Gan shows a groom with two horses. Later owners and experts added the seals and inscriptions.

Writing and paper-making

People started writing in China around 1800 B.C. The Chinese drew picture symbols to represent objects, instead of using an alphabet. Over time, these symbols, or characters, became simpler and looked more like designs than pictures.

Like other calligraphers, Buddhist monks continue to write in the traditional way.

Writing was developed for practical reasons, but Chinese artists saw that the characters were beautiful, too. They started practicing calligraphy, or the art of beautiful writing. They first wrote on bamboo, wood, and silk, until paper was invented in China, probably during the second century B.C. Paper was not very popular until A.D. 105, when a courtier officially informed the emperor of its invention.

The basic tools of a calligrapher were ink, an ink stone for crushing sticks of dry ink, a soft writing brush made from deer, goat, or wolf hairs, and paper. These became known as the four treasures of the scholar's studio. Painters liked to use silk, but calligraphers preferred paper.

Oracle bones

Around 1450 B.C., people were writing on animal bones and tortoise shells. They did this to find out about the future. The examples that have been found are called oracle bones. Special ceremonies were held when diviners, who were like fortune-tellers, scratched questions on the bones with sharp metal points. They then heated the bones in a fire so that cracks would appear. They read the cracks, which they believed were the answers from the spirits of ancestors. Sometimes they recorded the answers on the bones, too.

Useful bamboo

Chinese craftworkers used bamboo as a writing material in two ways. Before paper was invented, they wrote on strips of split bamboo. They bundled the strips of bamboo together to make an early form of book.

This tortoise shell was inscribed and allowed to crack.

Later on, craftworkers soaked strips of bamboo in water for a hundred days. Then they pounded the bamboo to a pulp and boiled it with lime for eight days. Next, they poured the mush into a vat and carefully lowered a screen into it. When they lifted out the screen, it was covered with a sheet of wet fibers. They pressed and dried the sheet, which became a form of strong paper.

Make your own lantern

Legend says that the first year of the Chinese calendar was 2637 B.C.
Since then, the calendar has counted years in cycles of 12. Each of the
12 years is named after an animal, in this order: rat, ox, tiger, hare, dragon,
snake, horse, sheep, monkey, rooster, dog, and pig. The millennium year,
2000, was the year of the dragon; 2010 will be the year of the tiger.
Chinese New Year celebrations start at the second New Moon after
the beginning of winter, between January 21st and February 20th.

An ancient lantern
festival takes place
15 days after the
New Year. Children
carry paper lanterns
to light their way into
a happy future. In
China, red is the color
of luck and happiness.

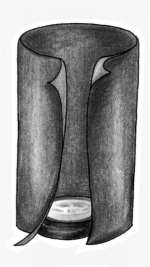

Make a paper lantern

You will need: a round oatmeal carton lid (about 6 inches
[16 cm] in diameter) • thick cardboard • red paper • strong glue
or glue stick • lightweight white paper (7 by 20 inches [18 x
50 cm]) • green, yellow and orange tissue paper • silver foil
• florist's wire • a bamboo rod • a ruler • a pencil • scissors.

1 The lid forms the bottom rim of the lantern. Before making the top,
measure around the lid, so the rims are the same size. For a 6-inch (16 cm) lid,
cut a 21-by-1-inch (52 x 2 cm) cardboard strip. Tape the ends together. Cut a
piece of red paper 10 by 21 inches (25 x 52 cm). Allow extra for a seam.

2 Spread out the red paper and decorate it. Tear the tissue paper into pointed strips, up to 10 inches (20 cm) long, and crunch up small pieces of silver foil. Stick the tissue streamers on to the red paper with the peaks pointing upwards. Add clusters of foil stars.

3 Cut a strip of white paper 20 by 7 inches (50 x 18 cm). Pleat the paper by folding it forwards and backwards in strips about 2.5 inches (6 cm) wide. Draw half a child against the folded edge and cut around the outline (but not into the fold). Open up the strip and a row of children will be holding hands.

4 Glue the cut out children 1 inch (2 cm) above the bottom of the red paper. Stick the paper around the outside edge of the bottom lid. Then put glue around the top rim and wrap the top of the lantern around it. Close the lantern by sticking the sides together with glue.

5 Add a colorful fringe. Glue thin strips of tissue paper to the inside of the lower rim. Make two holes opposite each other in the top rim and pull a length of wire through them. Bend the ends and twist the wire into a loop in the middle. Slide the lantern onto the bamboo rod and join the lantern festival.

Sculpture for temples and tombs

Chinese stonemasons and sculptors made large statues of people and animals to guard and decorate temples and tombs. They never made sculptures of the ancient gods, or emperors and empresses. Imperial rulers were shown mainly in silk paintings.

In ancient China, sculptors were craftworkers who used hammers and chisels. They were not as important or respected as those who used a delicate brush, who were seen as scholars as well as artists. This changed after Buddhism arrived, when sculptors began making thousands of images of the Buddha and his followers (see page 5). Some of these Buddhist statues were enormous.

A small section of the Terra-cotta Army beside the tomb of Shi Huangdi. They are standing in the pit where they were discovered. The clay figures were originally painted in army colors.

Stone qilin statues have guarded imperial tombs from around A.D. 450. This one stands at the tomb of Wu Zetian, the only ruling empress in Chinese history, who died in A.D. 705.

The Terra-cotta Army

Shi Huangdi, the man who called himself the First Emperor and ruled from 221 B.C. to 210 B.C., was worried about his safety—both in life and in death. He built a huge tomb to protect himself in the afterlife. Hundreds of thousands of craftsmen worked on the tomb, which included a model army of more than 7,000 life-sized clay soldiers and wooden chariots. The soldiers were mass-produced in separate pieces in clay molds. Skillful sculptors then made each one look slightly different so that every figure was unique.

Lions, dragons, and unicorns

Real animals, such as lions and turtles, as well as mythical ones, such as dragons and unicorns, guarded tombs throughout the Chinese empire. One of the most popular mythical animals was the *qilin*. This animal is sometimes called a unicorn; it has the head of a dragon and the body of a lion or deer, as well as small wings. People thought that the *qilin* brought good fortune. They also believed that a *qilin* appeared to the mother of the great philosopher Confucius, who was born in 551 B.C.

From silkworms to embroidery

Chinese legend says that silk was discovered in 2700 B.C. The discovery was made in the palace gardens of a ruler named Huangdi, who asked his wife Xilingshi to find out what was damaging his mulberry trees.

Xilingshi saw that worms were eating the mulberry leaves and spinning shiny white cocoons. She took some cocoons into the palace to study them and dropped one into hot water. To her amazement, a delicate, gauzy tangle came away from the cocoon, which was made of one long slender thread. Xilingshi had discovered silk. She took more cocoons and wove a robe for her husband and started the fashion of fine silk clothes.

The cocoons that Xilingshi found looked like this. They are spun by silkworms, which are caterpillars of the silk moth. A caterpillar changes into a moth inside its cocoon.

This 12th-century painting is a copy of an earlier work. It shows ladies of the imperial court stretching and ironing a roll of woven silk. The picture itself was painted on silk.

The Chinese guarded their new secret well, and for about 3,000 years, only they knew how to make silk. They used it for clothes, banners, and kites, as well as for writing and painting.

Spinning and weaving

When the cocoons are soaked in hot water, strands of silk separate and can be pulled away and wound onto reels. The ancient Chinese made wooden reels and spun strands together to make stronger silk thread. They built looms for weaving the thread into silk fabric. Women were in charge of the spinning and weaving, and they produced all kinds of beautiful fabrics. These were prized through the Chinese empire and the world. To the west, trading routes crossed deserts and grasslands to reach central Asia and eventually the Mediterranean Sea. They came to be known as the "Silk Road."

This silk robe was made in China more than 100 years ago. It was embroidered in the traditional, ancient style.

Embroidery

Silk was used for the finest clothes, as well as embroidery and tapestry. Craftworkers dyed silk thread in brilliant colors. Embroiderers used hemp or another coarse cloth as a backing. They drew an outline of a design on the hemp in ink, and then sewed the picture in silk. The finest Chinese tapestry was called *kesi* (meaning "cut silk").

Make a kite

No one is sure who invented kites. But we know they were flown in China thousands of years ago. There is a story that in 478 B.C. a Chinese philosopher spent three years building a kite in the shape of a hawk. Later Chinese emperors used kites to send signals to their armies. Early kites probably had a bamboo frame and were made of silk.

Chinese children love flying kites, especially on the ninth day of the ninth month, which is traditionally called Kite Day.

Make your own kite

You will need: two 24-inch (60 cm) wooden dowels • a craft knife • a cutting mat • 160-foot (50 m) kite string or fishing line • strong sticky tape • a large plastic trash bag • a cardboard tube • a ruler • a pen • scissors • poster paint • liquid dish soap.

1 Cut one side and the bottom of the trash bag and spread it out flat. Mark out a six-sided shape with a ruler and pen. Make sure that the shape is no longer than the dowels. Cut out the shape.

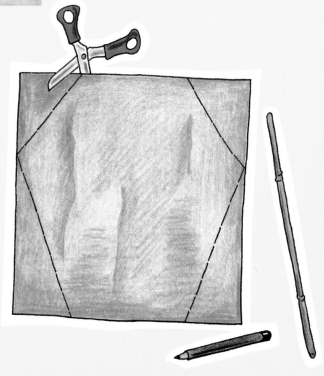

2 Put a round object about 2 inches (5 cm) in diameter near the bottom of the kite and draw around it. Move it 2 inches (5 cm) to the side and draw around it again. Cut out the circles. These vents make the kite stable in the air.

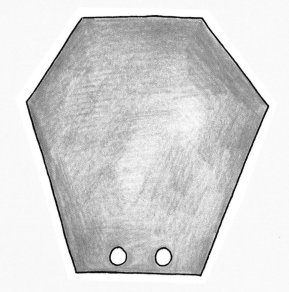

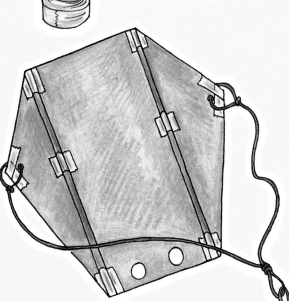

3 Stick the dowels to the plastic with strong tape at both ends and in the middle. Strengthen the kite corners with two pieces of tape. Pierce a small hole in each corner where the sticky tape meets.

4 To make the bridle (the line joined to the flying line), cut about 9.5 feet (3 m) of kite string. Thread the ends through the side holes and tie them securely. Knot another loop in the middle of the bridle. Then tie the flying line to the loop and wind the other end around the tube.

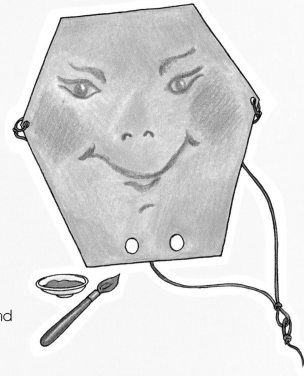

5 Paint a happy face on the kite. Poster paint mixed with a few drops of liquid dish soap will stick to plastic. Ask a friend to help you launch the kite. The friend faces the wind and holds the kite about 100 feet (30 m) away. You stand with your back to the wind and make sure there is no loose string on the flying line.

Pottery and porcelain

The earliest Chinese pottery, such as the examples found at Banpo (see pages 5 and 6), was made from clay. It was baked hard by being fired in a kiln. We call this kind of pottery earthenware.

This stoneware jar dates from around 300 B.C. The shape, design, and small handles are all similar to bronze cast jars of the same period.

Later Chinese potters coated the clay with a thin layer of glass, called a glaze, to make their pots waterproof. They then began crushing certain kinds of rocks into powder and mixed this with the clay before making their pots. These pots were called stoneware. They were waterproof and could also be used over a fire for cooking. Finally, around A.D. 200, the Chinese started making a third kind of pottery called porcelain, and this is the pottery China is most famous for. They made porcelain from white clay mixed with powdered rock. Porcelain pots were fired in a very hot kiln. When this fine pottery was brought to Europe, it was called "Chinaware." Porcelain is still called "chinaware" today.

Practical pots

In ancient China, most pottery was made for practical use and not for decoration. Pots were easier to make than bronze vessels and were used for cooking and as containers for food and drink. Potters used the shapes that metalworkers had been using for centuries. Potteries also produced figurines and other objects which were used in burials.

China from China

Chinese potters became masters in the art of making fine porcelain. Chinaware became the second most important export along the Silk Road. The best porcelain was white, hard, and smooth. In China, people said that it was "whiter than jade and thinner than paper." There was nothing like it anywhere else in the world and, as with silk, the Chinese kept their methods secret for many centuries.

This porcelain drinking horn in the shape of a lion's head was made in north-central China about A.D. 600. The potter probably copied its design from silver goblets made in Persia.

Lacquerwork

Lacquer is a kind of varnish that gives a smooth, hard surface to wood and other materials. The Chinese were the first to use this substance, which they made from the sap of the lacquer tree that grows in China.

This round box was made and lacquered during the period of the Han dynasty (206 B.C.–A.D. 220). It was painted with scrolls and inlaid with silver.

Ancient craftsmen learned how to tap lacquer trees and collect the white sap. They strained and heated the sap until it turned into a brownish syrup. They thinned this to make it runny, and added pigments to color the lacquer. Red and black were the most common colors. From around 1500 B.C. onwards, craft workers put lacquer on wooden and bamboo surfaces, as well as on metal and leather. The varnish added shine and decoration to the materials and made them waterproof. The secret of successful lacquerwork was to brush on many thin coats, adding each one when the previous layer was dry. Expert craftsmen sometimes put on 30 layers of varnish.

Working together

Many different craftsmen worked on a single piece of lacquerware. First a woodworker made the base shape. Next a craftsman brushed the first thin layer of lacquer all over the surface of the wood. This took days or even weeks to harden, since the bowl was kept in a damp place so the lacquer would not crack. After several more layers of lacquer had been added, a master craftsman brushed on the top coat. Then an artist painted and polished the bowl. This lengthy process needed large workshops where each craftsman looked after one stage of the process, working on a large number of bowls at one time.

To Korea and Japan

Many pieces of Chinese lacquerware were made more beautiful and valuable by inlaying them with precious materials. These included gold, silver, jade, ivory, and mother-of-pearl.

Lacquerwork became popular in neighboring Korea after 108 B.C., when China took over the northern half of the Korean peninsula. Chinese knowledge of lacquerwork and other crafts also spread to the islands of Japan. Before long, the Koreans and Japanese developed their own methods.

A modern artist works on a piece of lacquered furniture. Some Chinese companies still follow traditional techniques and designs that were used in ancient times.

Make your own lacquered bowl

Ancient Chinese craftsmen applied lacquer to furniture, coffins, musical instruments, and even house timbers. They also used it for their plates and bowls. Many were placed in graves and tombs. They were beautifully painted, mostly in red and black, with dragons, snakes, fish, and birds as decorations.

This lacquered bowl was made at the time of the First Emperor. In ancient Chinese art, fish meant wealth. The phoenix bird was a symbol of grace and power and often represented the empress.

How to make a lacquered bowl

You will need: a plastic bowl for the mold • glue • newspaper • toilet paper or tissues • white, orange, red, and black poster paints • brushes • varnish • vaseline for greasing • fine sandpaper.

1 Lightly grease the inside of the mold. Tear a sheet of newspaper into small pieces, soak them in water for a few minutes, and lay them on a sheet of newspaper. Cover the greased mold with a layer of damp paper, brushing the pieces down. Tear more newspaper into 1-inch (2 cm) strips.

2 Dilute the glue with water until it looks like thin cream. Line the bowl with overlapping newspaper strips and brush glue over each layer. Cover the bowl with 8 layers of paper. Smooth it down around the corners and press it against the sides so there are no air bubbles. Let the edges hang over the bowl. Leave it to dry for up to 2 days.

3 Take the dry bowl out of the mold. Trim the edges with scissors and remove any loose paper. Give the bowl a final layer of tissue, smoothing out any wrinkles. Cover it inside and out. Stick on the tissue with diluted glue and leave it to dry.

4 Rub down the bowl with fine sandpaper and paint it with white paint. Wait for it to dry. Mix red and orange and paint the bowl. When it's dry, copy the phoenix. Use a fine brush and black poster paint for the outline and add a black pattern around the rim. Varnish the whole bowl for a lacquered finish.

You could give the bowl to a friend—the phoenix is supposed to bring happiness.

Glossary

A.D. (short for "Anno Domini," or "in the year of the Lord"). This shows that a date is after the birth of Christ; A.D. 100 means 100 years after the birth of Christ.

archaeologist A person who studies the ancient past by digging up and looking at remains.

B.C. (short for "Before Christ"). This shows that a date is before the Christian era (which is called A.D.); 100 B.C. means 100 years before the birth of Christ.

bronze A metal that is a mixture of copper and tin.

Buddhism A religion based on the teachings of the Buddha, who lived in the sixth century B.C.

calligraphy The art of beautiful writing.

cereal A grass grown for its grains, such as barley, millet, rice, or wheat.

cocoon The silky covering that protects a caterpillar while it changes into a butterfly or moth.

courtier An attendant at a royal court.

diviner A person who predicts the future; a fortune-teller.

dynasty A series of rulers from the same family.

earthenware Clay pottery that has to be glazed to become waterproof.

embroidery The craft of decorating cloth by sewing patterns with colored thread.

envoy A person sent somewhere to act on behalf of a ruler or government.

excavate To dig up (in a search for ancient remains).

figurine A small figure or statuette.

fire To put pottery into a kiln to be baked hard.

glaze A shiny, glassy coating on pottery.

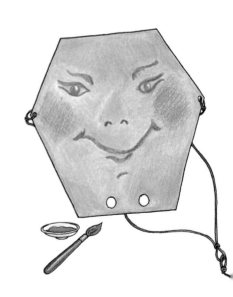

grave goods Objects put with bodies in ancient graves.

hemp A tough fabric made from fibers of the hemp plant.

imperial court The household of an emperor or empress.

ink stone A piece of stone on which sticks of dry ink were crushed.

kiln An oven used for firing or baking clay pots.

lacquer The sap of the lacquer tree used to coat wood and other materials.

lacquerware Lacquered objects.

master craftsman A very skilled and experienced craftsman who supervises the work of others.

millet A fast growing cereal grain.

mineral A solid chemical substance that occurs naturally in the earth.

missionaries People who travel to teach others about their religion.

nomads People who move from place to place rather than living in permanent settlements.

pigment The natural color of plants or other substances that can be made into powder and used in painting.

porcelain Fine white pottery made from white clay mixed with powdered rock; also called china.

stonemason A craft worker who shapes and prepares stone.

stoneware Pottery made from clay mixed with powdered rock.

terra-cotta Unglazed, hard, baked clay used to make pottery.

varnish Lacquer.

Index